Short Stuff

A Compilation of 444
four-line poems

by

C. L. Post

authorHOUSE®

AuthorHouse™
1663 Liberty Drive
Bloomington, IN 47403
www.authorhouse.com
Phone: 1-800-839-8640

Published by AuthorHouse 9/7/2012

ISBN: 978-1-4772-4818-8 (sc)
ISBN: 978-1-4772-4817-1 (e)

Library of Congress Control Number: 2012913015

*Any people depicted in stock imagery provided
by Thinkstock are models, and such images are
being used for illustrative purposes only.
Certain stock imagery © Thinkstock.*

This book is printed on acid-free paper.

*Because of the dynamic nature of the Internet, any web
addresses or links contained in this book may have changed
since publication and may no longer be valid. The views
expressed in this work are solely those of the author and do
not necessarily reflect the views of the publisher, and the
publisher hereby disclaims any responsibility for them.*

Dedication:

Most of the credit for organizing this book should be given to my friend, Mary. Mary's husband, Jay, passed away recently and it is to the both of them that I'm dedicating this book. Without her help, this book would not have been possible.

Contents

Introduction:

There are a lot of poems in this book. I hope you pick and choose your favorites from the selection. For you stalwart readers, you may read the book in one sitting, but if you so desire – read awhile – let some soak in and continue on later. The topics are many, the poems are short, thus the title:

Short Stuff

I hope you enjoy.

C. L. Post

Short Stuff

I hope you like
My book of poems
May they be something
That keep you going.

During the production of this book I had to have a wisdom tooth removed. We hope the wisdom itself wasn't lost!

Each of these poems
Is a work of art
I hope interpreting them
Will help to make you smart.

PROFESSIONAL PROWESS

My Friend Mary

I really couldn't do this
Without the help of Mary
I think that without her
I would not get very – far.

A Job

Some are full of hard labor
Others barely pay
But in reality you realize
It's the job that makes the day.

Business

If you're in a business
That's really on the edge
It's kind of like looking over
The boundary of a ledge.

Blockhead

If into a wall
You're being lead
Make sure you're not following
A real blockhead.

Learning in School

You learn to add
With all the rules
There are many things
To be learned in school.

School

School is an adventure
You swim in a great big sea
I learned and did a lot of things
In fact it taught and developed me.

The Whistle

That whistle in the distance
Is coming from a train
You probably won't hear it
Until it comes back again.

To Flex

Some say that stability
Will keep one in check
But what's good for flexibility
Are the muscles that flex.

Football

Football's a game
Where you cannot be lame
Usually it's strength and skill
That creates the thrill.

Hard Work

All the work it takes
To make it to the top
It's enough to drive one crazy
In fact it makes many stop.

A Day Off

Working really hard
With no time to sloth
Can't wait much longer
To take a day off.

Wise Men

Don't forget
A day's work – a day's pay
Is always what
The wise men say

The Question

You may have a neighbor
Who thinks he has the answer
But if he really doesn't
Is slamming doors the answer?

Hammer and Nails

With all the doubt
About things that may fail
Look to solid structures
Built with hammers and nails.

Chores

When you're beginning
Your daily chores
Rest up before you
Hit the floor.

Dust

Dust is a problem
And dust you just might
Stir up the dust
That collects with the night.

T.V.

Today it's the daily
Broadcast
That delivers the news
Of the outcasts.

Film

Pictures that move
And that are taken
Is film that cannot
Be mistaken.

The Police

When fighting crime
You need a friend
There's no better friend
Than the local policemen.

Scraping the Bottom

I'm digging for ideas
But they just don't seem to come
This is the part of writing
That really isn't fun.

Goodbye

When you're trekking down that road
You break the way you pave
So remember when departing
To give a great big wave.

The Centerline

When driving you follow
The centerline
Stay right, drive straight
And you'll be fine.

Salt

Salt's white and it's bitter
And comes out with a shake
But with butter and flour
A recipe it makes.

Revisiting

When visiting
It's fun to relate the facts
When revisiting
You can often rehash those acts.

Relaxing

You don't have to be lazy
To stretch out and rest
Remember to take time
And relax with the best.

WEATHER
WORDS

Space

The Solar System's big
And its planets travel around in rings
The galaxy's even bigger
And the universe contains everything.

Sunlight

Streaming in
This Monday morn
It's sunlight that
This day does form.

Sunshine

Bright, beaming and warm
The rays of the sun are sent
But when a shadow appears
You may wonder where they went.

Dusk

Just before sunset
All over town
Dusk settles in
As the sun goes down.

The Answer

If love is the answer
Remember to try
To bring out the sunshine
In a cloudy sky.

Puffy Clouds

Clouds like pillows
Sky of blue
With the wind
Just passing through.

A Cloud

Some are round and puffy
Others long and straight
But a cloud is a cloud
With a message to relate.

Rain

From the clouds
Down comes the rain
It will stop
Till it comes again.

Raindrop

Holding to the windowpane
Gripping to the branch
Falling from the cloudy sky
Missing what's to chance.

Raindrops

Raindrops falling
On the fly
Why can't we see them
Returning to the sky.

April 1st

By the first of April
Spring is usually the rule
But you can't outguess Mother Nature
She doesn't raise any fools.

Hurricanes

These and typhoons are called
The kings of the storm
It's over warm water
That these monsters are born.

The Weather

The weather today
Is clear and near 70
When the weatherman's wrong
It's a calamity.

Azaleas

Roses with their thorns
Often times will nail ya
But the beauty of the spring
Can be seen in the azalea.

The Bud

Spring brings the warmth
The warmth that won't leave
Sprouting the buds
Upon all the trees.

Blades of Grass

This green substance
Can grow quite tall
So cut your blades of grass
Rather small.

Water

Clear and wet and quenching
Falling from the sky
Mixed with herbs or coffee
You drink it with some pie.

Breeze

With the wind
Comes the breeze
If you get chilled
You may have to sneeze.

The Fan

If you're hot and sweaty
And stuck on dry land
Remember to always plug in
That trusty fan.

The Swim

On a hot summer's day
If you get a whim
Remember that there's nothing quite like
A cool water swim.

Summer Swim

In the summer it's nice
To be close to the water
If you haven't been swimming
Then really you oughter.

End of Summer

Lazy August days
Coming to a close
Was it only 8 months past
That we nearly froze.

The Rake

As leaves blow
We use the rake
Or a leaf blower
For those who ache.

Snowflakes

Floating from the sky
Each an individual
Landing on soft powder
Taking its place on schedule.

Blanket of Snow

Although it's 10 degrees
And the wind does blow
We'll still stay warm
With this blanket of snow.

BUSY-NESS
BI-LINES

The Journal

News – news – from all around the world
What will they think of next
Some news is good – some news is bad
Boy is this world perplexed.

Medicine

For that cough
Or even the flu
Just rustle up
A big bowl of stew.

6:00 AM

Eight in the morning
Head full of bricks
Just think what you'd feel like
If it was quarter to 6.

What We See

Look around
Take a peek
The world around us
Lasts more than a week.

The Vase

Flowers alone
Look out of place
It's times like these
That you should put them in a vase.

Foraging

Looking for food
Is the job of the beasts
It would be hard not knowing
From where came your eats.

Taking a Break

Whether taking a break
Or just having fun
Remember; get your rest
So you can get your work done.

Brewed Coffee

Sitting around
Not much to do
So take a sip
Of your favorite brew.

Time Travel

Time seems to travel
Sometimes slow or fast
But there's really nothing you can do
For the time that has just passed.

Standing in Line

If you're first, you won't wait long
Because you're in a lucky space
But if you're last and have to wait
You wish someone would take your place.

Scissors

Two blades that cut
Material to paper
We need a pair of scissors
On the caper.

Funny Money

When one takes lightly
The scope of economics
Then the nature of life
Will be left up to the comics.

Bumming It

When your activities
Seem to stop
Let's hope you don't
Begin to flop.

Necessities

If all that was needed
Was a banker and money
Then why on earth
Isn't every day sunny?

Bull Market

Business is busyness
When it works like a charm
This is true especially
Down on the farm.

The Situation

Corporations form
The megalopolies
While others ask
Are they good company.

People Problems

With too many asking
"Is there enough to go around?"
It begins in a sense
In your little town.

Department Stores

If you're looking for a bargain
But you don't really know what for
Just take a friendly visit
To your local department store.

Memories

When sitting around the campfire
In the great outdoors
Don't forget the memories
Or the stories told with s'mores.

This and That

If all we know is this and that
Then what are we to recite
When this and that become something new
Then you are said to be bright.

The Streetlights

Lighting the night
When no one's around
They sure do brighten
This little town.

Jelly Jargon

If you were Jack in the Beanstalk
Would you ever be seen
Making a jar of jelly
By planting a jelly bean.

If You're Last

When you're all alone
Can't talk to a soul
Follow the wires
Of the telephone pole.

Replenishing

When you've reached
The barrel's bottom
Remember to refill it
Every autumn.

The Rent

When it comes to paying bills
You should do it in a flash
Because what it takes to pay the rent
Is a sum of cold, hard cash.

APROPOS APPAREL

Patches

Patches are made
To cover a hole
They're also the areas
That generate coal.

Fabric

Needle and thread
Can bring you to stitches
And these are the knots
That hold up your britches

Blue Jeans

Blue jeans come in many sizes
They are the rave at school
Once only worn by farmers
Jeans make you really cool.

Threads

You look kind of nice
In your new threads
You look rather handsome
Is what some people said.

Proper Attire

When wondering whether
To weather the storm
Remember to remember
What clothes should be worn.

Raincoats

If you need something
To keep off the rain
Then buy a raincoat
Be it fancy or plain.

Rainwear

Some like beards
Some like mustaches
Some like boots
Others galoshes.

Rainsticks

You'll be stepping in style
A proper young fella
When you walk in the rain
Beneath your umbrella.

Handwarmers

They're not just for winter
Or the people we love
There are many different styles
And colors of gloves.

Mexican Sombrero

With a maraca in one hand
You'll know where you're at
When you show up at the party
In your mariachi hat.

Oldies but Goodies

Button your buttons
And shine your boots
You'll be stepping in style
In your fancy Zoot Suit.

The Fashion

Showing those long legs
No need to flirt
Remember this when you're
Wearing your mini skirt.

New Suit

Whether to church
Or a meeting you go
You'll look the dapper
In a new suit you know.

Sporting Jacket

Whether it's kind of quaint
Or loud with all that racket
Remember that when traveling
To wear your sporting jacket.

Talk of the Town

Some are white
Some tan or brown
But when wearing a trench coat
You'll tear up the town.

The Topcoat

If all you need
Is something over the top
Then look to the topcoat
Before money you drop.

A New Hat

Spring has arrived
I bid winter adieu
I've bought a new hat
I may even buy two.

Belt

If you're holding your pants up
With your hands, rope, or suspenders
Just get yourself a belt
It's a cinch when you pay the tender.

Socks

Socks come in many colors
Some look like this and that
But the ones that give you trouble
Are the ones that don't match.

Shoes

Shoes on your feet
Cover your toes
Some have no shoes
Is that how it goes?

Shoestring

Some use buckles
Some use rings
But what holds mine on is
The old shoestring.

New Shoes

If you're feeling down
And really have the blues
To get out of the doldrums
Just put on some new shoes.

Two Shoes

Two shoes, new shoes
Is what we used to sing
But who in this great big world
Would buy the ones with wings.

Slippers

Some come with string
Some come with a zipper
Is there anything close
To the comfort of a slipper.

The Pipe I Smoke

The pipe I smoke
Is made of briar wood
I don't smoke it much
Although I could.

THOUGHTFUL THEMES

Once

If it doesn't happen
Then you can say never
But once upon a time
Is really pretty clever

The Headwaters

At the mouth of a river
Going into   the sea
You look upstream and wonder
Where the   headwaters could be.

Keep Trying

If the topic is trying
Reach for   the sky
Because it took many years
For man to fly.

2 Cents

Two cents won't make you rich
For those who have none
But one thing is for certain
It's better than one.

Fast Food

If you need a
Quick, easy dish
Rustle up
Some tuna fish

Modern Laundry

Laundry blowing
Flapping in the breeze
These days with dryers
We do our laundry with ease.

Reason for Being

With all the knowledge that we possess
Who'd even wonder why we'd question
The reason for life on this great earth
For some it's merely perception.

My Friend

I met a friend in the store today
He had a word to say
He's been a friend for quite some time
And still is to this day.

Rings

Rings on your fingers
Rings on your toes
In Africa some people
Have rings through their nose.

Clipping Your Nails

Clipping your nails
Will make you look better
But combing your hair
Is the real eye-getter.

Pressed for Time

People in a hurry
Are often pressed for time
And if they wouldn't worry
Things would work out fine.

Antennae

If all you receive
You'd like to delete
Just bring in your antennae
So the signals don't repeat.

Reaching for Peace

Reaching for peace
Reaching high and low
Reaching for peace
Is the only way to go

The Hammer

If Bob Dylan had a hammer
He'd hammer in the morning
Sometimes those that hammer
Don't give any warning.

A Lamp

If you need light
Turn on a lamp
Remember the wattage
And even the amps.

The Planter

Holding its pot
Which is drawing the center
Of the talk of the plant
That resides in this planter.

The Plant

It's green with seed
And leaves avast
I'll water this plant
So it may last.

Hands

The clock ticks on
With its outreached hands
To measure the time
We spend on this land.

The Cowboy

With brands and lassos
Roping the cattle
Is the roaming cowboy
Still in his saddle?

The Rudder

In deep water
Or if you're a mudder
Remember to always
Steer with your rudder.

Thunking

When thinking of thought
Remember it's thunk
And probably has already
Been stashed in a trunk.

A Leaky Pen

Nothing makes you more angry
Than a leaky pen
After you clean yourself up
You have to start over again.

Both Ways

If the train
Is coming down the track
There's usually another one
That has to go back.

Rain

Even as the world goes round
We know it's going to rain
This is because of the even keel
That Mother Nature has on this plane.

Signs

You should do
What the sign says
Just look where you've been
And where the signs have led.

ANIMAL ANNALS

Pets

Nothing compares
To the warmth of a ferret
Unless it's the beautiful
Colors of a parrot.

The Horse and the Blacksmith

The horse for so long
Did the work of the land
There was for every hoof
A man to lend a hand.

The Raccoon

With the darkened eyes
Of the pesky raccoon
It's hard to tell
When one's in the room.

Squirrels

Looking for a peanut
Is the neighbor squirrel
If you happen to spook him
He'll scurry about in a whirl.

The Elephant

If he has big ears
And really funny toes
He's an elephant 'cause
He has a trunk for a nose

Stripes

If you can't tell
Whether it's coming or going
It must be a zebra
With its stripes all knowing.

The Bear

They roam about
Without a care
It's hard to trace
The wanderings of a bear.

Counting Sheep

If in your sleep
You see one leap
Don't speak a peep
You're only counting sheep.

Bobcats

In Ohio
There used to be a slew
Now all the bobcats
Reside at O. U.

Flying Cows

They speak of the cow
That jumped over the moon
But what ever happened
To the dish and the spoon?

Your Dog

Dogs have keen ears
Some have big tails
A dog is the friend
That never fails.

Dogs

Lazy dogs lay
Other dogs play
But my mangy mutt
On dog bones does prey.

9 Cats

They say a skinned cat
Has 9 lives
Is this the truth
Or a bunch of jive.

For the Birds

Up upon a wire
A line of birds is strung
Feeding at the feeder
They take their turns at the wrung.

Little Ones

One little peeper
Strayed from the nest
I'm not so sure
What happened to the rest.

The Parakeet

If it's a squeak
You hear from its beak
Be it strong – be it weak
It's the sound of the parakeet.

The Cuckoo Bird

The stories they'd tell
If we only knew
The true flight
Of the cuckoo.

The Gold Fish

Every kid's had
A goldfish true
And when it was flushed
It made him blue.

Fish

If it's a meal
You'd like in your dish
You can go out and hunt
You can go out and fish.

The Fox

If one of these
You catch in a box
Then it's for sure
You outsmarted the fox.

The Scorpion

Walking through the desert
You wouldn't suspect a thing
But beware of the scorpion
With its poison sting.

The Rattler

Water and grasslands
Are the homeland of the snake
Although on hot rocks
The rattler does bake.

The Tortoise

As a pet
You may have had a turtle
Which in its true sense
Is a tortoise with a girdle.

Spiders

Some spiders are small
Some are gargantuan
But the hairiest of them all
Is the tarantula.

The Skunk

If sometimes you
Smell a little funk
Look around
It may be a skunk.

UNTITLED
POEMS

I left the following four-line poems untitled. The reason for this was not because I couldn't come up with titles, but because I want the reader to read each poem, think about the thought, subject, or feeling each exuberates and to put their own thoughts or ideas as the title for each poem. Sort of a reader participation. Now stimulate those thoughts and proceed.

Sundrops drip
On rainy days
It's these that
Bring us through the haze.

Leaves leave the tree
Each fall
And come back in spring
To all.

Chimes ring in the sound
Of the wind
Only to blow its sound
Once again.

Rain brings water
Sun brings heat
We need these two things
For what we eat.

When nothing seems
To go your way
Remember tomorrow's
Another day.

If clouds bring rain
And thunder clap
It's kind of hard
To take a nap.

Grass grows green
At least it should
In a dry spell though
It almost turns to wood.

Shoes shuffle us along
With our feet in them
Bringing us people
With the reasons to meet them.

The captain's the boss
The crew does the work
Unless there's a mutiny
On the little jerk.

If one has only pennies
And saves them in time
Those pennies will soon
Grow into a dime.

Rays of sun
Shine through the leaves
It's these spring days
For which I am pleased.

Once we're through trying
Things will get done
It's accomplishing things
That brings the fun.

Because we are people
We're put here to love
So say hello to your brother
And all the others you think of.

Prices seem to be rising
This is because inflation is growing
We need to prick it with a pin
To know where the aim is going.

Round and orange
You'd think it was the sun
But it's only a basketball
And why little kids want one.

If for once
You think it's over
Remember to continue
It's better than clover.

Although you may
Become weary
The trip will be
Well worth it.

A footprint
Tells two things
Where one goes
And what one brings.

Just because
Or just what for
Are two little sayings
You should restore.

Clean socks
Are like a clock
When they get dirty
They need wrung.

Lunch bunch
With a hunch
Is a group of
Chatterers.

Frozen lakes
Seem to call
For the ice skater
In us all.

Candle's glow
Shimmering light
Breaking the barriers
Of the night.

Snug as a rug
But if you give a tug
You may find you're loose
As a goose.

Fill your cup
To the brim
If it's enjoyment
You pour in.

Paper a plenty
With nothing to do
Writing the topic
That pleases you.

Flowers look pretty
And smell twice as sweet
When given to friends
And the people we meet.

Jugs that are full
With a story to tell
It's the jugs that are empty
That are the ones that are swell.

Dice have 6 sides
Yet they lie flat
If you roll box cars
Roll again where they sat.

Hair that is styled
Is hair that has class
So bring on the stylist
For the hair on that lass.

When the breezes begin to blow
And stir up this and that
One thing that you need
Is the proper hat.

Boxes for clothes – boxes for shoes
Boxes can hold anything
From something that's old
To something that's new.

MORE
UNTITLED

Endings are sad
Though they bring memories
It's the beginning that leads us
To what we can see.

Whether telling a fable
Or just an old yarn
Remember not to let
The cow out of the barn.

Boxes are square
Wheels are round
It's a good thing that they're
Not the other way around.

Brushing brings brightness
Combing comes clean
After going to the barber
You're something to be seen.

Because the sun shines
The flowers bloom
When it's dark at night
There's the light of the moon.

Clouds bring us shade
And sometimes they rain
But do they really
Deserve all the blame.

It looks like fun
Feeding a monkey a grape
But feed him too many
And he turns into an ape.

Some are cantankerous
Others just rotten
If it's a comment
From an old man you've gotten.

Time slips by
It doesn't try
To reason why
It seems to fly.

A hat is cover
For one's head
Some heads need covered
Enough said.

Plants are green
And grow small or tall
It's into the poison ones
That you don't want to fall.

Snow lies low
Unless it's on a roof
And in the blazing sun
The snow goes poof.

To remember
What we see
Is to literally
      – Be.

Once or twice
Maybe again
It's after these
That we begin.

Tick Tock
Goes the clock
The things it would say
If only it talked

Lines are sometimes crooked
Other times they're straight
The lines that are on this paper
Are the lines I try to relate

If the head of the band
Is the leader
Is his helper
The Band-Aid?

If you take the time
Things will get done
But it's up to you
You are the one.

At times you may wane
At times you may slack
At times perchance
It's inspiration you lack.

Every day without fail
The sun does come up
So make a pot of coffee
And have another cup.

Though the hours seem long
And time seems to last
Just think how fast the day goes by
And the week that has just passed.

Water is great to drink
It really quenches our thirst
But think of all the water we'd have
If the dam that's holding it burst.

Think of all the luck we have
Because of this earth we're on
And of all the gold being guarded
By those tiny leprechauns.

Sometimes winter's a hinder
And summer's a bummer
But spring's the thing
Till fall – that's all

Learning to walk step by step
Is something we all do
But learning to sleep and rest our heads
Seems to be something we always knew.

If spring never came
There'd be such a stir
'Cause soon it would be summer
That would come in a blur.

The sun shines down
On this green earth
And each spring it brings
A new rebirth.

Even if the sun doth shine
And the rain begins to fall
Would you see the rainbow
And the good of things in all.

Usually in the winter months
Most of us lie low
But in the spring and summer
There's plenty of grass to mow.

The wheel of life
Goes round and round
Just look at all
The spokes you've found.

Jumping jacks make
One healthy
A pair of jacks make
One wealthy.

Nickel, quarter, dime
All make up the dollar
If the penny's ever worth anything
Give me a holler.

HOLIDAYS

Holiday

Everything's closed
No mail today
As we all celebrate
This here holiday.

New Year's Day

The year that's past
Is the year that's been
On New Year's Eve
Ring the New Year in.

Martin Luther King Day

Martin Luther King
Set the standards high
We should all attempt to reach them
At least we all should try.

Groundhog Day

Usually a groundhog
Has nothing to say
Except for the one
On Groundhog Day.

St Valentine's Day

St. Valentine's day
Brings chubby Cupid
Whoever said
Love can be stupid.

St Patrick's Day

On St. Patrick's Day
You must make the scene
Because on this day
Everyone is green.

Easter

Easter is a blessing
For without it you all know
That if our sins weren't paid for
To hell we all would go.

Memorial Day

A day for those who gave
The greatest gift of all
To build this country to what it is
Our young brave soldiers fall.

The 4th of July

The day of birth
Of this great land
Comes on the 4th
Strike up the band.

Labor Day

A day of rest
For those who toil and labor everyday
It's honoring our accomplished works
Why we celebrate and play.

Thanksgiving

The Indians and Pilgrims
Soon became good friends
They held a feast for the hungry
When the crops were in.

Christmas

Santa perched
Upon his sleigh
Christ was born
On Christmas Day.

STILL MORE
UNTITLED

Here is a second group of untitled poems. Be wise, creative and use your literary freedom to label each unnamed poem.

Some of our toes are big
Some very little
The toes that are average
Are the ones in the middle.

As the wind blows past
On a warm summer day
It makes the leaves rustle
Like they have something to say.

Quietly tip-toeing
Not making a sound
You'd never know
That anyone was around.

Everyday is special
Which is brought on by the sun
So remember to accomplish something
Then go out and have some fun.

Night brings out the stars
And perhaps a planet or two
If it weren't for the batteries in our flashlights
What on earth would we do.

In daylight we can see
What lies ahead each day
Though some of us remain in the dark
It's not to be that way.

When quenching that thirst
You might have a beer at first
But what does it for me
Is a nice tall glass of tea.

A screwdriver and a wrench
Can fix most of our troubles
But you may have to use the phone
To sometimes call a plumber.

When you get that hunger
For a burger and some fries
Don't forget dessert
Perhaps a piece of pie.

Umbrellas in the wind
Can really be a pain
But they sure do come in handy
When there's a gentle rain.

Holding hands they say is sweet
And could lead one into love
If one only knew what this could bring
Some would wear a glove.

If coffee's on the menu
It may take the lead
Because after you've enjoyed a cup
It brings you up to speed.

Once a flower blooms
Its fragrance is released
It's the pollen and the fragrance
That really draws the bees.

Winter is a bummer
With coats and scarves and boots
Just lead me to the summer
Where the foliage plants its roots.

If everything had a name
Each horse would have a bridle
But this isn't always the way it is
Take this poem and its title.

Some homes come as bargains
Others with strings attached
But always give me a loving home
Where the door can be open or latched.

The brain does all the thinking
The mouth relates the tongue
If everything is in working order
A beautiful song is sung.

Drops of water
Drops of ink
Can you stop the drops
That are in my sink.

Some work hard
Others loaf
Bakers are the ones
That can do both.

To a little girl
There's nothing like a doll
They create magic and imagination
Even if they're small.

Dragging along
A flexible flyer
Your troubles will go
As the hills get higher.

Coal is dark and dirty
And is usually in a mine
But in the winter when it's cold
It heats the room just fine.

The price of gas is rising
And will be like a balloon
But what I think we're waiting for
Is a down market to show soon.

If for once
You get another chance
Remember this time
Not to lose your pants.

Cars can be fun
That is if they run
But cars that go fast
Usually don't last.

Time runs down
And passes by
This is why
We should always try.

Hail is just ice
That look like small stones
But when they get large
They do damage and wreck homes.

A candle's wick
Will hold the light
It blows in the wind
But holds on tight.

The wind will whisper
Its mysterious tales
But you should head for cover
When it begins to gale.

Some drive down the road
With ease – not even knowing
Some travel to their destination
Not thinking where they're going.

When painting a house
Remember it's best
If the sun is shining
To take a rest

The sun is the center
Of our solar system
So if he didn't come up
You must have missed him.

LAST OF THE UNTITLED

Words are easy
Words are neat
In communication
Words can't be beat.

Listening to the music
On the radio
Gets one in a happy mood
Lifting your spirits don't you know.

Flowers whether in a pot
Or on a mountain growing wild
Will get you in a pleasant mood
And make you feel like a child.

If you're in the dumps
And you need a lift
Just remember the words of a friend
And trust them like a gift.

Some birds live in houses
Some birds live in nests
I like when they're on the wing
And think these are the best.

If you're in the great outdoors
Sitting around a campfire
Remember it's days like these
Of which you never tire.

When jogging it's nice
To see all the sights
When racing it's plain
To see that winning's the gain.

A pair of pants, as a gift
Be they jeans or be they knit
Are only well appreciated
If they have that proper fit.

If we only knew
What lies ahead
Then we would know
To where we're led.

When you're down on your luck
And you can't fix your truck
Pull out a buck
And get out of the muck.

If it rains in Spain
It falls mainly on the plain
If it rains in Missouri
Would we have to worry?

Billy's got a fever
Anna's got a spell
Mama's taken the bucket to see
If there's water in the well.

Dark skies
Big clouds
Thunder claps
Pretty loud.

Snow builds up
Until the Spring
Then there won't be
Anything.

Sledding is not
For faint of heart
Because the top of a hill
Is where you start.

Black coffee is good
Hot or on ice
When drinking a cup
Remember to pour twice.

If it's refreshment you want
And a thirst you must dash
Remember to always
Begin with a splash.

Once it's been said
Words have been spoken
The trick is to keep your word
And not get it broken.

If for a lack of words
One seems to act out
Remember sometimes it's better
To give a little shout.

Some dogs are black
Some dogs white
Beware of dogs
That take a bite.

Picnics are fun
On fair days
But when it rains
There's no place to play.

When riding a bike
Remember to steer
Or you may hit
Things that are near.

If your neighbor's shouting
Scat – scat – scat
It may be because
Of the neighborhood cat.

If you were wondering
About eating a paw
Remember to get
A good sweet bear claw.

When things seem to go
Past pretty fast
Remember the things
That seem to last.

Once it's done
You shouldn't undo
Unless what you've done
Doesn't please you.

Lines on the ceiling
Lines on the wall
Just where would we be
If there were no lines at all

When one meets two
It could make three
This is why I'm here
It happened to me.

When you're in a jam
Drink a bottle of beer
It will stimulate your thought
And break those cobwebs drawing near.

Just because you're there
Means that you're not here
Sometimes we're afraid
Because of our own fear.

Keep that body moving
No matter what age you be
Because as we all get older
It's movement we like to see.

After scrubbing up
From your toes up to your face
Remember to always put
The soap back in its place.

When we breathe
We fill our lungs with air
But go and ask a fish
And they won't even care.

This marks the end of the untitled poem section of my book. I hope you enjoyed the poems and placed your own title, if only in your mind, to the poem's ideas, subjects and thoughts. If you just breezed through them, then sometime in the future go back and try to title a few. It's a lot of fun.

The rest of my book contains six more chapters of titled poems.

Keep on trucking, you're almost there.

WISE
WORDS

On Top of Spaghetti

Mushrooms and cheese
And sauce if you please
With spaghetti and meatballs
There's nowhere to sneeze.

Food

Corn grows ever higher
Soybeans stay small
What would we do
If there was no food at all?

Candy

To curb your appetite
Try a little candy
It's sweet and tastes good
In fact it's kind of dandy.

Toast

Till it becomes toast
Bread is merely bread
But if it's toasted; darkened
It becomes crunchy instead.

Crumbs

Some get a good slice
Others fight for the loaf
But you'll be left with the crumbs
If your bread is burnt toast.

A Bag

If you were to carry things
So others won't nag
You might entrust the use
Of what we call a bag.

Playing it Safe

If someone bothers you
Get a look at his face
The clothes he's wearing
But don't give chase.

Needed Company

When in doubt
Rely on the help of a friend
They give good advice
And always have a hand to lend.

Time to Think.

If something happens
And you're on the brink
Remember to relax
And take time to think.

Our Brains

As we sit and wonder
The wheels of the brain churn on
They spark our imaginations
And solve problems we're working on.

To Read

Words on paper
Not in your head
That is of course
Till they've been read.

Rhyming a Word

Rhyming a word
Or the last syllable is great
Sometimes it's there
But other times it ain't.

All Rhymed Out

When you seem to think
That ox will rhyme with boulevard
I think it's time to quit
Because you're trying much too hard.

Learning Something New

If at first
You don't know the song
Don't give it up
Just follow along.

Language

Remember it takes each letter
To make up a word
And in every sentence
Is a subject and a verb.

The Painting

Be it landscape or portrait
Classical or modern
Painting is a craft
Where you can get your art in.

A Walk

If you're stir crazy
You shouldn't balk
Just pick a path
And take a little walk.

Time

Time keeps on ticking
As it passes by
You can never catch it
Even though you may try.

Things That Seem to Be

Some things change
Some things stay the same
But what we really see
Are things that seem to be.

A Whole Hole

A hole
Isn't a hole
Unless
It's whole.

Because

If, maybe, or what's up
Are all thoughts to contemplate
But if you act out just because
What's the point that you'd relate.

Penny or a Nickel

Penny or a niclel
Quarter or a dime
No matter what you're saving
It all adds up in time.

Sitting on a Gold Mine

If you're sitting on a gold mine
It's best to let it set
'Cause when it's gone, it's gone
And you'll wonder where it went.

Once

Once there were
And this is true
Things that were known
By only a few.

Weather

Weather is something
That the weatherman knows
But whether weather weathers
Is in which way the wind blows.

QUAINT
QUOTES

My Pen

Some pens are idle
Some pens scribble
But when my pen writes
It writes for a nibble

To Write

Once it's wrote
They say it's written
This; by the writing bug
I've been bitten.

Titled

Writing a word upon a line
May not seem like very much
But write a few and make a phrase
And your sentence will have that touch.

Paper

When writing one must say
The pen is very unique
But without paper to write on
Your hopes become very bleak.

Love of Writing

Writing by far
Is fun if it's clear
Writing with love
Is writing that's near.

Babies

One thing is for sure
Babies are the best
They still have their innocence
And an outlook that is blessed.

The Bowl

Cereal or rose
Each are a bowl
Then there's the kind that comes with shoes
And a ball that you roll.

Peppercorn

Salt comes in shakers
And flour in sifters
A grind of peppercorn
Will make you sneeze if you're a sniffer.

Making Good Decisions

If you're in trouble
Or just in the drudge
Remember the one
Who's always the judge.

Love

A long lost love is one that is
Never forgotten through the years
And renewing the feelings of the past times
Brings smiles as well as tears.

Things to do

Even though the end is near
Remember to look through it
When you're done with the things you're doing
There'll be more if you just get to it.

Coasting

Once your vehicle
Starts its ride
Just sit back
And enjoy the glide.

The Bus

If you need a ride
That will take all of us
Just buy some tickets
And get on the bus.

Offroad

When you're off road
And hitting the ruts
Aren't you glad
Your wheels have lug nuts.

One Diet Coke

One diet coke
Is all that I'll drink
It quenches my thirst
And helps me to think.

Tea or Coffee

For those who toddle with their drinks
I suppose the talk is over tea
But if in fact you're of the rougher sort
The subject may be coffee.

Glass

Holding water tightly
Brimming to its fill
Drink a glass of water
Hoping not to spill.

Clean Towels

After wiping up the mess
You made just the other night
A hand towel in the wash
Will make everything all right.

A Candle

Sitting in the dark
Is something some can't handle
So for a little light
They might strike up a candle.

Becoming Dusty

Dust can gather
Very fast
If things are left
In their past.

Life's walk

If everything were
As easy as was said
Would our walk through life
Take us where it's led.

Life's Experience

If you just do nothing
And let the time go by
You will not progress in life
So please, give living a try.

Weather II

Air is circulated
By high and low pressure
And temperature changes
Are what affect the weather.

Wise Men

Once there was an old man
Who had a lot to say
If only I could experience
What he has – up to this day.

Reason for Life

Of all the things that we possess
In fact – the nature of this reading
Is to stimulate and relate to our souls
The facts that life is feeding.

PEOPLE POEMS

Progress

Before the paper
Before the phone
Sometimes it's nice
To be left alone.

Single

Single is not coupled
This is what some men say
So far for me, that is
I've been single to this day.

Hair

It can be short
Or it can be long
You can be a redhead
Or even a blonde.

Muscles

Some are strong
Then become sore
When you weigh 98 pounds
You wish you had more.

The Rubdown

Sore muscles the problem
Ben-Gay around
Spread it all over
And get a rubdown.

Breakfast

Breakfast really is
The most important meal
If you don't have it
You won't know how you feel.

On the Road

Wherever there's people
Don't you know
There's always traffic
On the road.

Writing on Russia

Russia is a country
That is really very large
You can reach it by flying airplane
You can even take a barge.

Big Stuff

Some people don't
Know who they are
Till they light up
A big, good cigar.

Friends

Friends who are true
Are friends to the end
Friends will no break
But at times they may bend.

Heroes

Heroes can be rock stars
Or even the man on the street
But most of the heroes I know
Have achieved some sort of feat.

Mothers

Mothers are the greatest
Seems like they're always there
And those that make the best mothers
Are those that really care.

Brothers and Sisters

Brothers are really something
Sisters maybe three
If it wasn't for the family
Where in the world would we be.

Good Friends

Dear friends are priceless
When you're down and out
They come running to help
And you don't even have to shout.

Girls

Girls are a gas
Whenever they walk past
In fact it's quite clear
Whenever one comes near.

Friends II

If you're ever in a jam
And you need some relief
Remember that a friend to lean on
Is as good as roast beef.

Carefree

Some drive down the road
With ease – not even knowing
Some travel to their destination
Not thinking where they're going.

Progress

Centuries ago
We traveled by wagon
Today if we walk a mile
We're usually saggin'.

Cityfied

If you grew up in the country
You know how the crow flies
But some need a G.P.S.
If they're cityfied.

Peculiar People

They say there's nobody
Crazier than people
They'll even drink booze
At a bar with a steeple.

Footsteps

Wherever you go
You follow your feet
It's these leading footsteps
On which you repeat.

Worms

Be they red and small
Or big, brown and fat
Fish – like a little kid
Seem to know where the worms are at.

Stealing

Sometimes the unwanted
Who stick around and linger
Will eventually be tempted
To use their sticky fingers.

The Mic

Remember if you happen to say
Something someone might not like
To always be sure to
Turn off the mic.

The End

If one's down on their luck
And one needs a friend
Remember the one
Who's a friend till the end.

MEMORABLE
MOMENTS

The Flag

If you're behind
And sometimes seem to lag
Remember to keep up
And always fly your flag.

Summer Days

Some days wane
Some days want
I'm spending this day
With my aunt.

College

College is fun
But you learn a lot too
In fact it's the first place
Where you can be you.

The Bonfire

Root for the home team
Flames a'roaring higher
If only we could understand
The leaping flames of fire.

The Bleachers

They contain different types
Of many different creatures
When you root your team to win
You're usually in the bleachers.

Elvis

Elvis was the king
He liked to sing and dance
If he was still alive
Would he wear those fancy pants?

Great Memories

The things you remember
Are the things that rate
So try to remember
The things that are great.

The Ticket

The shows are a showin'
They're right in the thicket
But before you go in
Remember your ticket.

The Movie

The show is a screening
So give it a peek
They'll show you some previews
Of what's on next week.

Pictures

From motion to still life
Each picture holds the truth
If you've ever taken a bad one
You know this is the proof.

Moving On

All life's work cannot be measured
By the rank that one has gained
Because for each of us the starting point
Is different from the point that one attains.

Travel

Staying in one place
Can really get on your nerves
As for me I long to travel
All the straights and all the curves.

Las Vegas

Vegas is great
For those who play slots
But for some it's a menace
It takes everything they've got.

Winning

When one has accomplished
His appointed aim
Then this is the time
When you've won the game.

Accomplishments

If for lack of want
Or lack of money
Remember the sweetness
Is in the honey.

Placemat

When dining you usually
Sit where you're at
And the thing that catches your drippings
Is the good old placemat.

Ice Cream

I like ice cream – yes I do
The question is do you?
If you are in fact like me
The question is one scoop or three.

Sure Sweetness

Sugar in your coffee
Can be quite a treat
But is the sugar in the bowl
Only half as sweet.

The Quake

Earth shattering – mind boggling
Continental shelves on the move
Trapped people scramble
And the Red Cross sends food.

Repetition

If we were only to
Repeat what we see
Where in the world
Would our history be?

Misplaced

Don't you just hate it
When something is misplaced
It slows you down a little
And takes you off your pace.

B-Ball

B-Ball is a fantastic game
It's played for fun and pleasure
And all the enjoyment and benefits of playing
Cannot even be measured.

Broadcasting

Baseball has been very good
At least for those who play it
And to all those who are the fans
The broadcasters are apt to relay it.

Snowstorm

Just when you think
Your ducks are in a row
A storm whips up quick
And you're covered with snow.

Nighttime

With dusk setting in
We tend to bed down
This is usually done
All over town.

SUITABLE
STANZAS

Ears

We have two
Upon our heads
It's to these ears
That sound is led.

A Gazer

You may wonder many things
When gazing at a star
You may wonder where you're going
You may wonder where you are.

Our Earth

On earth – some places are hot
Some places are cold
But it's the rocks on the earth
That really make it old.

A Letter

Messages are related
Whenever a letter is sent
You place it in the mailbox
Knowing where it went.

Jazz

If it's morning
And you can't sleep
Wake up to
That jazzy beat.

The Banana

The banana is long and yellow
And is quite good to the taste
It even has an organic peel
That will recycle back as waste

Cream

White as the lilies
Cream is the best
When mixed with coffee
Its taste takes a rest

Ketchup

It's merely squashed tomatoes
But really tastes superb
When put on a hot dog with relish
An appetite it curbs.

If Only

You can answer a statement
With, "If Only!"
But if you do
You're full of bologna.

The Color Blue

Red's rather bright
And shines rather true
But if I buy a car
I think it might be blue.

Roses

Petals so soft
Their silk divine
Some are white or beige
Others red as wine.

The Tree

It stands there sturdy
As it has for years
If you're in the woods
You know that one is near.

Tires

Tires carry the weight
They keep the grip with their tread
It's the rubber to the road
That serves to get you ahead.

Batteries

Flashlights can't glow without them
Toys can't entertain without them
Radios won't play without them
How do we get along without them?

A Chair

When you need to get off your feet
With that certain flair
Pick the most comfortable position
And sit down in a chair.

The Grovelers

Problems never seem
To be as bad as we think
But there's always certain people
Who put up a big stink.

The Switch

You can turn on a light
Or even scratch your itch
These days; merely by
Flipping a switch.

Saturday Nights

You know it's time
To lay off the throttle
When everyone at the bar
Is looking through beer goggles.

Ashtrays

Ashtrays alone
Recepticate the ash
It's the cigarettes that really
Burn up the cash.

Bottle of Wine

Arbors in position
Grapes upon the vine
Soon it will be time
For that fine bottle of wine.

The Flow of Words

Whether reading or rhyming
Whether to oneself or aloud
The flow of the words
Is what makes oneself proud.

Striving

When nothing seems
To fit the bill
Reach deep inside
For your self-will.

70

70's your lucky number
When playing bingo heaven
But for the luck of the Irish
Put your money on 77.

Sleep

You may just be
Resting your peeps
Then again you may be
Going to sleep.

The Simple Life

It's the simple pleasures
That get us through life
Don't let things get you down
Shed the trouble and the strife.

FORMIDABLE
FORMATIONS

Headlight

Mounted on the front
It's big, it's bright, it shines
Bringing light to darkness
This beaming bright fine line.

Light

Light can be filtered
To look many ways
Most light is white light
Which we see everyday.

Darkness

As we look
Into the fading light
It's the darkness that turns
The day into night..

Stars

Looking up you only see one
That is if it's during the day
But looking up at night, it's then that you'll see
Where all the stars seem to stay.

The Shovel

When making a hole
Or spreading the gravel
You need a handy shovel
With a good handle.

A Dirty Floor

A dirty floor
Is sometimes a sight
The dust seems to collect
Because of its height.

The Frame

Square or rectangular
Holding in place
Pictures of people
With smiles on their face.

Paper

Paper is one thing
On which to write or fold
Working with paper
Never gets old.

Italy

Italy's known for many things
Including the Mona Lisa
But will they ever straighten up
That Leaning Tower of Pisa?

Corner

2 lines meet
At what angle
Now there's a corner
That you've fandangled.

The Bridge

If there's a valley
Between two ridges
Sure enough
There's probably bridges.

The Streetcar

Streetcars used to
Rule the land
Whatever happened
To the streetcar plan.

To Look

Sights for sore eyes
Are sights for to look
Sights that bring happiness
Are sights that are took.

The Procrastinator

If you wonder why you're behind
Or why you're usually late
You may be subject to procrastination
That always makes you wait.

A Cup

When measuring for a recipe
You should use the ingredients up
To get the proper proportions
Be sure to use a cup.

Climbing the Ladder

Changing your scenery
You move to different spaces
To get up in the world
You climb to higher places.

Spending Money

Some have credit cards
Others ready cash
Still others go right through
Their fortunes in a flash.

Learning

School is quite important
It's really where you learn
It keeps the body active
And lets the old brain churn.

A Hyphen

If you join words
Or run out of space
Remember to put a hyphen
In its proper place.

Education

They say it's worth the money
That's what some people say
But I say it's what you know
That gets you through the day.

Music

If the sound is soft and mellow
Or even it it's loud
Music can soothe the body
And make one feel very proud.

The Dandelion Flower

You're a flower
Yet you're a weed
You reproduce
By going to seed.

The Spruce

If there were a tree
So straight and true
It would have to be
The spruce that's blue.

The Elm

If there were a tree of the forest
That was at the helm
It would undoubtedly be
The mighty elm.

Running out of Words

Nothing is as stunning
Without nouns or even verbs
As is coming to the end
And running out of words.

The End

This is the last poem
Contained in this book
So go back now
And take another look.

This book was written mainly, to prove that, in some cases, a lot can be explained in a short manner. Short Stuff is, I admit, a rather simple book with rather simple poems. But taken individually each poem expresses its ideas in a miniscule moment.

I hope you derived something from the many poems offered in this book and, if nothing else, received some pleasure in reading them.

Dedication:

I would *also* like to dedicate the poems in this book to my elementary school principals, teachers, cafeteria workers, and janitors.

Principals: Mr. Lane and Mr. Carr.
Kindergarten: Mrs. Brown
First Grade: Miss Vioni
Second Grade: Mrs. Thomas
Third Grade: Mrs. Flood
Fourth Grade: Mrs. Collins
Fifth Grade: Mrs. Lindstrom

And after switching schools:
Sixth Grade: Mrs. Cleveland

Also a thank you to Mrs. Shonk and the cafeteria workers who kept us fed and to Mr. Vargas and the janitors who kept the schools spotless. We didn't know how good we had it. Thank you for your dedication and inspiration and I hope you see a little of what you taught us in my book.

Thanks again, C.L Post

Little Known Facts about C. L. Post

Attended nursery school.
Learned to ride a bike after the training wheels fell off.
Played YMCA Flag Football.
Once froze a snowball to throw in the summer.
Fell out of his tree house.
Quit the freshman basketball team.
Likes artichokes with mayonnaise.
Wore a top hat to the high school prom.
Graduated high school with a "C" average.
Worked at a steel mill.
Won his college football intramural championship.
Was cut from his college varsity football team.
Went on a 250 mile canoe trip in Canada.
Likes salt on his vegetables.
Graduated college through the mail.
Worked at a Hilton Hotel.
Published first book in 2001.
Visited Tucson, Arizona.
Started CraigLPost.com website.
Loves cantelope.
He also hopes you enjoyed this book.

-- Until Later

Personal Notes

Personal Notes

Personal Notes

Personal Notes

Personal Notes

Personal Notes